# STEWART Hamster

The author and publishers are grateful to
Mr Andrew Grant, Vet M.B., M.R.C.V.S., for his
advice during the preparation of this book.

British Library Cataloguing in Publication Data

Snell, Nigel
  Stewart's hamster.
  1.Pets. Hamsters. Care
  I. Title    II. Series
  636′.93233

  ISBN 0–340–50019–0

First published in 1989

Published by Hodder and Stoughton Children's Books,
a division of Hodder and Stoughton Ltd,
Mill Road, Dunton Green, Sevenoaks, Kent TN13 2YA

Printed in Belgium by Proost International Book Production

A FIRST PetCare BOOK

# STEWART'S
# Hamster

## BY NIGEL SNELL

HODDER AND STOUGHTON
LONDON SYDNEY AUCKLAND TORONTO

## A present for Stewart

Stewart and his Mummy are going shopping to buy Stewart's birthday present. He wants a pet hamster.

The pet shop is full of puppies and kittens, rabbits and birds. The hamsters are at the back. There are several different kinds. A few are plain white, and a few are brown and white, but most are a beautiful golden colour.

*Choosing a hamster*

Stewart likes the golden hamsters best. 'May I have that one please?' he says, pointing to a frisky little hamster with bright black eyes.

Mr Fish gently lifts the hamster out of its cage and puts it into a cardboard box, ready for Stewart to carry home. The box has holes in it so that the hamster can breathe.
'This is a female hamster,' says Mr Fish. 'She's eight weeks old today.'

'Then I'll call her Octavia,' says Stewart.

## *Buying a cage*

'Octavia will need as large a cage as possible,' says Mr Fish. 'Hamsters are active little animals and need room to exercise. It's also a good idea to give them an exercise wheel like this one, fixed close to the cage wall.

'Hamsters like plenty of cage "litter" for burrowing. In the wild, hamsters spend much of their time in underground burrows. So when you get home put some hay, kitchen paper and cardboard in her cage which she can tear up for "litter".

'Hamsters also like a nesting box for sleeping in. The box should be lined with hay to make a nice soft bed.'

## Setting up the cage

Mummy buys a cage, some hay and some hamster food. Then she takes Stewart and Octavia home.

Mummy puts the cage on a table away from the window. Pet hamsters don't like direct sunlight. She puts a thick layer of sawdust over the bottom of the cage, and some hay, paper and cardboard on top.

Next, she fixes a water bottle to a cage wall. Stewart pours some hamster food into a feeding bowl and puts it inside the cage.

Finally, Mummy opens the cage door and guides Octavia inside.

HAMSTER FOOD

## Octavia's new home

Stewart and Mummy watch while Octavia explores her new home. She scurries along the edge of the cage and up the ladder to her nesting box. Then she climbs onto the wheel and pedals round and round. She makes quite a noise!

'I'm glad she's not in my bedroom,' says Stewart. 'She'd keep me awake all night.'

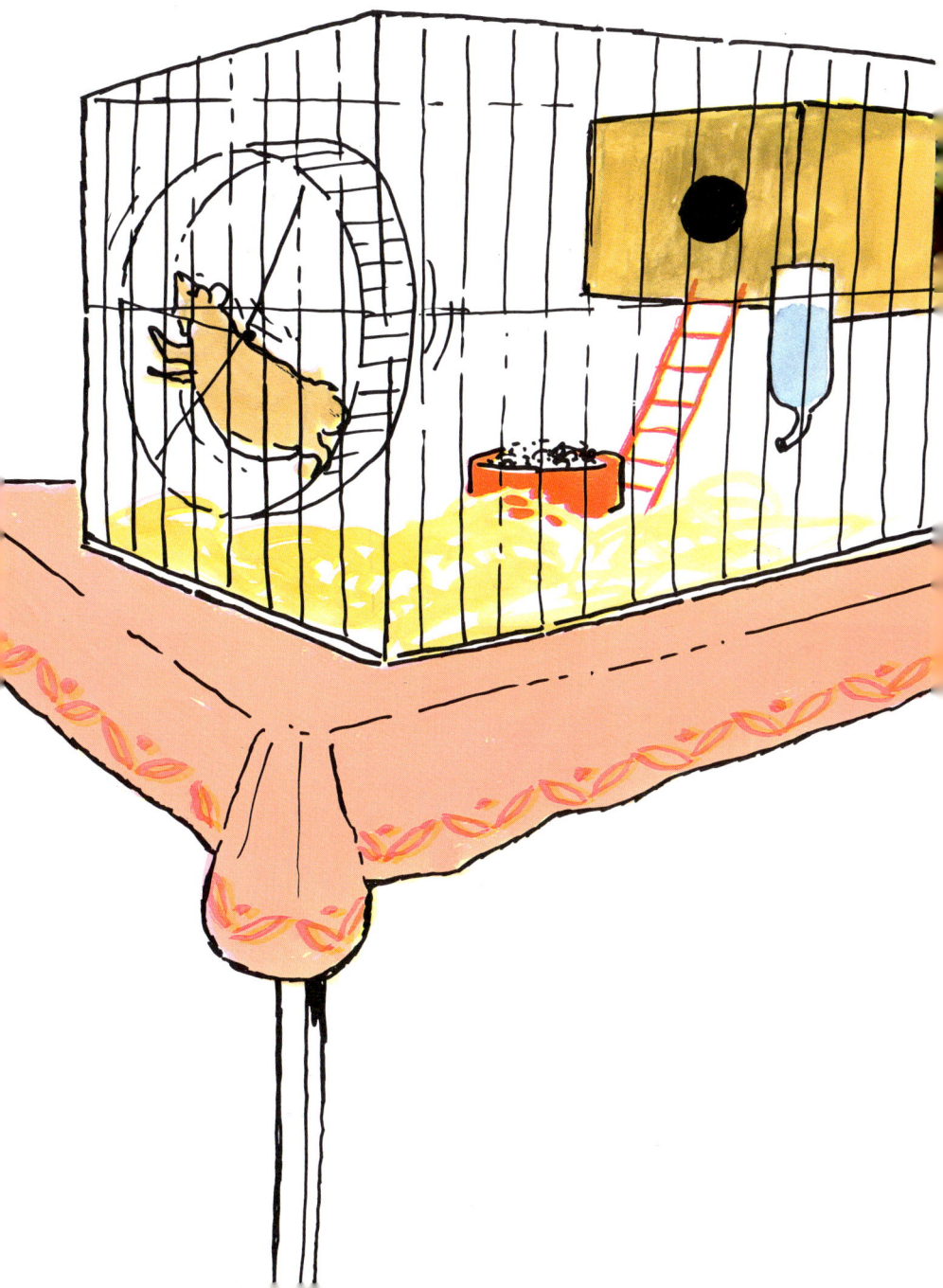

*Playthings*

Mummy says that hamsters soon get bored, so they need plenty of things to play with. Mummy puts an old cardboard tube and an empty cotton reel into the cage.
'Never allow Octavia to play with toys made of thin plastic,' Mummy warns. 'Her teeth are so strong she might break the toys and hurt herself.'

Mummy also puts a gnawing block into the cage. All hamsters need to gnaw in order to wear down their long front teeth.

## Feeding

Octavia nibbles at the mixed seeds, grains and nuts in her bowl. She seems to like them.

'Perhaps she'd like a little brown bread or dry porridge oats as well,' says Mummy.

Hamsters also enjoy fresh fruit and vegetables – for example, pieces of apple, pear, tomato, cabbage, carrot and swede. They also eat some plants, such as clover and dandelions. The plants should be well washed.

Now and again hamsters also like a slice or two of hard boiled egg, a piece of cheese, or some scraps of cooked fish or meat.

HAMSTER FOOD

Octavia doesn't eat her food straight away. Instead, she takes it into her cheek pouches and carries it to her food store to eat later on. Her pouches are quite delicate. They can easily be scratched by sharp seeds and other foods.

Octavia needs plenty of fresh drinking water every day. Stewart makes sure that her water bottle does not leak.

## A clean cage

Every day, Stewart helps Mummy remove Octavia's droppings and uneaten fresh food. Octavia is a messy eater and leaves food all over the place. He tops up her bowl of dry food and refills her water bottle. Then Mummy tells Stewart to wash his hands.

Once a week, Stewart cleans out Octavia's cage. He throws away the old sawdust and 'litter' and puts in some more. It is very important to keep her cage clean or she could become ill.

## Holding a hamster

At first, Octavia doesn't like being picked up. Instead Stewart gently strokes her inside the cage. A few days later, he is able to hold her in cupped hands.

Soon Stewart is able to lift Octavia out of the cage. He makes sure there is a table directly beneath her. Hamsters often jump if they are nervous or startled. If they land on the floor, they may easily run away.

## A healthy hamster

Hamsters normally stay healthy if they are fed properly and kept in a clean cage. But even clean, well-fed hamsters will become sick if they are not allowed to rest during the day. Both wild and pet hamsters are most active at night and during the early morning and evening.

In winter, when it is cold, hamsters normally go into a deep sleep. Stewart stops Octavia doing this by keeping her room nice and warm.

## Friends

Stewart and Octavia are soon firm friends. When Stewart lifts her out of her cage, she runs up his arm and sits on his shoulder. When Octavia is in her cage, he likes watching her run up and down her ladder or turn her wheel. He is very proud that Octavia is such a happy, healthy hamster.

# Index